MW01062699

PRAYER, PEACE
and the PRESENCE of
— GOD —

A 30-Day Journey to Experience the Shalom of Jesus

DAVID BUTTS

PRAYERSHOP
PUBLISHING

Terre Haute, Indiana

PrayerShop Publishing is the publishing arm of Harvest Prayer Ministries and the Church Prayer Leaders Network. Harvest Prayer Ministries exists to transform lives through teaching prayer.

Its online prayer store, prayershop.org, has more than 200 prayer resources available for purchase.

© 2017 by David Butts

All rights reserved. No part of this publication may be reproduced in any form without the written permission of PrayerShop Publishing, P.O. Box 10667, Terre Haute, IN 47801.

ISBN: 978-1-935012-80-1

THE HOLY BIBLE, NEW INTERNATIONAL VERSION®, NIV® Copyright © 1973, 1978, 1984, 2011 by Biblica, Inc.® Used by permission. All rights reserved worldwide.

1 2 3 4 5 | 2021 2020 2019 2018 2017

Contents

How to Use This Guide

Prayer, Peace and the Presence of God is not designed to be read like a book. It is a 30-day prayer guide, designed to be taken in daily doses. I encourage you to chew on the content of each day, pray over it, let the prayer and prayer point each day sink in to your soul. After doing that, throughout the day as the Lord brings back to mind what you read, continue to process it through prayer.

My desire is to see you learn to experience and walk in the shalom of Jesus through any experience, any trial, any stressful situation.

The Apostle Paul challenged the Philippian believers,

"Let your gentleness be evident to all. The Lord is near. Do not be anxious about anything, but in every situation, by prayer and petition, with thanksgiving, present your requests to God. And the peace of God, which transcends all understanding, will guard your hearts and your minds in Christ Jesus." (Philippians 3:5-7)

My encouragement to you is that as you lay your burdens and stresses at the feet of Jesus, you will experience God's peace and God's presence as a regular part of your ongoing walk with Jesus.

My hope and prayer for you is that after 30 days of focusing on Jesus' peace, walking in peace will be a way of life for you.

I also encourage you to consider using this resource with your entire church family. Imagine what a congregation could do, completely at peace with the Father!

—Dave Butts

Introduction

In peace I will lie down and sleep, for you alone, LORD, make me dwell in safety. (Psalm 4:8)

Because I am writing a devotional on peace, it's embarrassing to admit that sometimes I have some anxiety. It can especially hit me at night when I'm trying to sleep. If I'm not careful, it can develop into a full-blown panic attack. I feel like I can't stay in bed or I'll suffocate. There have been times when I find myself awake and pacing through the house in the middle of the night, trying to understand how a Christian who is supposed to walk in peace can experience such an appalling lack of it.

I'm not a psychologist who can dissect all the possible reasons for this, but in my own life, I know that sometimes, I simply have not accepted the peace of God into a place of permanence in my life. I can read scriptures that speak of peace without stopping and praying, giving God thanks for his peace and allowing his peace to settle into the very depths of who I am.

My prayer is that this devotional will help you to go deeper in practical peace than you have ever gone.

I would also suggest to you that sometimes the lack of peace is an outworking of the spiritual warfare that surrounds us. Jesus described Satan as a thief. One of the things Satan often tries to steal from me is peace. If my peace is only an emotional attachment, then it becomes easy for the enemy to steal it from me with just a bit of physical discomfort or stirring up my mind with thoughts not from the Lord.

So what do I do when I find myself wandering the house at night, unable to sleep because of a lack of peace? I go to the Word of God and begin to pray one of the many passages that speak of the peace of God.

God's Word doesn't present peace as simply the absence of hostility or some state of nirvana we achieve through meditation.

Instead, Scripture ties peace to the presence of God himself. That's why I believe that walking in peace becomes a clear sign of someone who is experiencing the revival that comes from God's presence.

One of my favorite scriptures to pray at night is Psalm 4:8. The very ability to lie down and sleep is one of the benefits of peace. Regardless of outward circumstances or inner turmoil, the peace of God gives us the ability to rest in him. This verse equates peace with the phrase, "for you alone, Lord." God's peace is the practical outworking of the Lord's presence in our lives. He is the one who makes us dwell in safety. This is an amazing gift of God that is to be accepted and embraced.

DAY 1

He Is Our Peace

For he himself is our peace, who has made the two groups one and has destroyed the barrier, the dividing wall of hostility, by setting aside in his flesh the law with its commands and regulations. His purpose was to create in himself one new humanity out of the two, thus making peace. (Ephesians 2:14-15)

In 1995, I had the great privilege of participating in the Global Consultation on World Evangelization (GCOWE) in Seoul, South Korea. Christian leaders from more than 100 nations had come together to strategize how to reach the world for Christ in our generation.

Of all the amazing things I experienced, one simple story stood out. I had lunch one day with two Christian brothers from Uganda. The two men were roommates and that was amazing. They were from two different tribes, the Hutu and the Tutsi. In those years, Uganda had been rocked by astonishing brutality as those two tribes warred back and forth in the cruelest ways. It was hard even to understand how such evil could happen. Virtually everyone from either tribe had someone in his or her family who had been murdered by the opposite tribe.

And yet, here they sat. Brothers in Christ, representing their nation, and even more, their Lord, on the other side of the world from their war-torn nation. They roomed together, ate their meals together, and as their story became known, they were walking parables of what the Prince of Peace does within the lives of those dedicated to him.

The Apostle Paul would have enjoyed meeting these two Ugandan Christians. They were illustrations of what he was trying to communicate to the Ephesians and to us regarding the astonishing power of the peace of Christ. The big division in Paul's day was between Jew and

Gentile. The early Church struggled greatly with how to bring such differing backgrounds, beliefs, and ethnicities together into one body.

The heart of Paul's teaching is that the heavy lifting of this task has already been done by Jesus. His death on the cross did something that no number of conferences, or seminars, or proclamations could have done. He himself is our peace. He made us one. Something happened on the cross that forever impacts our relationships with one another.

This passage in Ephesians is a good example of what N.T. Wright spoke of in his book, *The Beginning of the Revolution,* when he challenged us to rethink the purpose of the cross and see it as more than just the personal aspect of "saving us from our sin." Paul presents the death of Christ as the creation of one new man in Himself. The peace that Paul speaks of is supernaturally contained within Jesus himself and is made available through the cross to a divided mankind.

Now, that can all sound like theological musings until we connect it to my two Ugandan friends who learned to live out that supernatural peace in the midst of horrendous ethnic hatred. Think of the possibilities for Jew and Palestinian, Indian and Pakistani, or even liberal and conservative in the United States. And what about those who you are divided from in your own family, or neighborhood, or workplace? Jesus, through his death, has made available to us the peace that is in him, that we might live out that peace in the midst of a badly divided world.

My Prayer

Thank you Lord, for becoming our peace. In your death, you tore down walls that divide and made us into one new person who lives in your peace. Help us to live out what you have placed within us. May your peace be a passion within us.

Prayer Point

Is there someone with whom you have had difficulty? Begin to pray for God's peace to break down the dividing wall between you and that person.

DAY 2

Peace I Leave You

Peace I leave with you; my peace I give you. I do not give to you as the world gives. Do not let your hearts be troubled and do not be afraid. (John 14:27)

One of the more admirable traits of humans is our desire for peace. It just hasn't turned out well for us. We all know of peace talks and treaties that failed. In an older study (1894), Russian sociologist Jacques Novicow documented that from the year 1500 B.C. to 1860 A.D. (3,360 years) more than 8,000 treaties were adopted with intention to assure permanent peace. The average time they remained in force was only two years. Peace between humans is much sought after, but seems to be elusive.

Jesus distinguishes clearly the peace he offers with that which can be found in the world. In a very real sense, he renames this as "my peace." The peace of Christ must not be confused with the world attempts at peace. What the world reaches for, admirably, but in vain, is simply the absence of hostilities. What Jesus offers his followers goes deeper than that. His peace is a gift given by him to those who are following him. It is formed deep within us and transforms us from the inside out.

Jesus was about to demonstrate what he meant by his peace. When he was arrested in the middle of the night, abused and beaten, and forced to stand before authorities in a mockery of a trial, he appears to be the only one at peace. Others are shouting and upset. Jesus, who had every reason for distress and anger, stands in peace before His accusers. While outward circumstances seem to call for anything but peace, the Prince of Peace simply lives out who he is in the midst of chaos.

Jesus has left this peace with us. It is clearly a gift, not just for a few select disciples, but for all who follow him. That is so encouraging. It is to be received, embraced, and deepened through regular practice. The peace of Christ clearly does not promise us an absence of hostilities. In fact, Jesus promised us times of trouble (John 16:33). But because of his great gift of peace, he is able to say clearly to us, "Do not let your hearts be troubled and do not be afraid."

As it was for him personally, the peace of Christ shines brightest in times of adversity. It may be when your faith is on the line as it was for Jesus before the authorities. But there are many times of trouble that we face in this world. It could be the loss of a job, sickness you are facing, problems with a relationship, or the death of a loved one. When we turn our attention from our circumstances to the Lord over the circumstances, we will find the peace that is ultimately in him, given to us through his grace.

My Prayer

Lord Jesus, thank you for this amazing gift of your peace. You lived out this peace as you dwelt among us, and left it here for us. Help me to fully embrace your peace and live it daily. Especially in times of trouble, teach me to look to you and your peace rather than the turbulence in which I find myself. May my heart not be troubled, nor my fears overtake me because of the wonderful gift of your overwhelming peace.

Prayer Point

When you hear Jesus say that he leaves his peace with you, have you ever personalized that? Thank the Lord now, for giving you his peace.

References: Blog by S. Brian Willison, "The Failure of Peace Treaties." Jacques Novicow, *War and Its Alleged Benefits*, Translated by Thomas Seltzer (New York, 1911). Originally (Paris: A. Colin, 1894).

Peace Be with You

*"Do not be afraid, you who are highly esteemed," he said.
"Peace! Be strong now; be strong." When he spoke to me, I was
strengthened and said, "Speak, my lord, since you have given
me strength." (Daniel 10:19)*

Have you ever had such an amazing encounter with God that you thought you were going to die? Time and again in the Scriptures, we read of those who had such encounters. Without exception, there was great fear as they came into contact with God, whether it was Moses listening to God from a burning bush, or Mary receiving a message from the angel Gabriel.

The Prophet Daniel had one of the more spectacular encounters as he was given a vision of an angelic being, who in all probability was the Lord Jesus in his pre-incarnate state. The similarities of the description in Daniel 10 of the angelic being and the clear description of Jesus as seen by the Apostle John in Revelation 1 are striking. Daniel's response was to lose all strength and fall down before the Lord.

God dealt with Daniel's fear in ways that are encouraging to us all. He spoke his peace to Daniel and everything changed. God's peace always has that sort of dramatic effect in our lives. The Lord assured Daniel of his love for him and then spoke peace over him. More than words, the speaking of peace into someone's life becomes a conduit for peace actually to begin to flow into an individual's life. With the peace of God coming into Daniel's life, the Lord could speak of strength and courage, and it had real meaning to Daniel.

It was in this place of peace where Daniel was strengthened that he could finally summon the courage to ask the Lord to speak to him. Do you suppose that it is often fear and lack of peace that prevents us from hearing what the Lord might be saying to us? We so often play the "what if?" game, which breeds fear and uncertainty to the point that we really don't want to hear from God for fear of what He might say. His peace though, clears out those fears, brings strength, and puts us in a good place for the Lord to speak into our lives.

We often use the phrase, "paralyzed by fear." That's what fear does when it takes charge of our lives. We become too frightened to make decisions or to choose which way to go. Whether the fears are based on reality or fantasy is not even the issue. It is fear that prevents us from action. That's why we so often quote the words of President Franklin Delano Roosevelt as he attempted to calm the fears of a nation paralyzed by the Great Depression, "The only thing we have to fear is fear itself."

God has a supernatural way for us to deal with fear. It is accepting his peace into who we are. Receiving His assurances of love as Daniel did, we hear his words of peace and our fears begin to melt away. Strength comes as fears melt away, and peace resumes it rightful place over our heart.

My Prayer

Lord, I am so thankful that you understand the fears that I face. You don't ever simply tell me to get over it. Instead, you assure me of your love and give me your peace. I confess my great need for this in our day of confusion and turmoil. I desperately need the peace that only comes from you.

Prayer Point

Ask the Lord not to allow you to be paralyzed by fear but always to be strengthened by his peace.

Crush Satan under Your Feet

The God of peace will soon crush Satan under your feet. The grace of our Lord Jesus be with you. *(Romans 16:20)*

Somehow reading about the God of peace who crushes Satan doesn't seem to fit with our picture of peace. But if we're talking about a God who gives peace to his children, it makes perfect sense. Satan so often comes to steal peace. He creates and delights in chaos and confusion. The God of peace who desires for his children to walk in peace will step into this situation and crush the one who is stealing peace and bringing about distress. The Prince of Peace will indeed bring peace!

One of my heroes of the faith is Martin Luther King, Jr. He often faced chaos created by the enemy. In a sermon entitled "Our God Is Able," he shared in a very deep way how God stepped in to crush Satan under his feet and give King his peace.

Almost immediately after the Montgomery bus protest had been undertaken, we began to receive threatening phone calls and letters in our home. Sporadic in the beginning, they increased day after day. At first I took them in my stride, feeling they were the work of a few hotheads who would become discouraged after they discovered that we would not fight back. But as the weeks passed, I realized that many of the threats were in earnest. I felt myself faltering and growing in fear.

After a particularly strenuous day, I settled in bed at a late hour . . . and was about to doze off when the telephone rang. An angry voice said, "Listen, (expletive), we've taken all we want from you. Before next week, you'll be sorry you ever came to Montgomery." I hung up, but I could not go to sleep. It seemed all my fears had come down on me at once. I had reached the saturation point.

I got out of bed and began to walk the floor. Finally, I went to the kitchen and heated a pot of coffee. I was ready to give up. I tried to think of a way to move out of the picture without appearing to be a coward. In this state of exhaustion, when my courage had almost gone, I took my problem to God. My head in my hands, I bowed over the kitchen table and prayed aloud. The words I spoke to God that midnight are still vivid in my memory.

"I am here taking a stand for what I believe is right. But now I am afraid. The people are looking to me for leadership, and if I stand before them without strength, they too will falter. I am at the end of my powers. I have nothing left. I have come to the point where I can't face it alone."

At that moment I experienced the presence of the Divine as I had never experienced him. It seemed as though I could hear the quiet assurance of an inner voice, saying, "Stand up for righteousness, stand up for truth. God will be at your side forever."

Almost at once my fears passed from me. My uncertainty disappeared. I was ready to face anything. The outer situation remained the same, but God had given me inner calm.

Three nights later, our home was bombed. Strangely enough, I accepted the word of the bombing calmly. My experience with God had given me a new strength and trust. I knew now that God is able to give us the interior resources to face the storms and problems of life. Let this be our ringing cry . . . that there is a great benign Power in the universe whose name is God, and he is able to make a way out of no way, and transform dark yesterdays into bright tomorrows. This is our hope for becoming better [people]. This is our mandate for seeking to make a better world.

Taken from article by Ruth Haley Barton, "Martin Luther King, Jr and the Soul of Leadership." Found online at transformingcenter.org

How is Satan trying to steal your peace? What fears are coming your way that you don't know how to deal with? Are you looking for ways to just slip away and leave the battle to others? Follow the model of Martin Luther King, Jr. and so many others who have turned to Jesus and found the God of peace who will crush the enemy under *your* feet. Did you notice that? God doesn't crush Satan under his feet, but under yours. You begin to walk in his peace and his strength because of the overcoming power of Christ who has crushed the enemy under your feet. May the grace of the Lord Jesus Christ be with you!

My Prayer

Lord, I give you thanks for your overcoming power. You are the mighty One, King of Kings and Lord of Lords. Though you are the God of peace, your love of peace and desire for it in the lives of your people impels you to crush the stealer of peace, Satan, under our feet. Thank you, Lord, for providing that victory for us. Help me to walk in your victory and live out your peace in my life.

Prayer Point

When it seems like the enemy is attacking you, ask the God of peace to crush Satan under your feet.

DAY 5
An Honest Appraisal

*Even though I walk through the valley of the shadow of death,
I will fear no evil, for you are with me; your rod and your staff,
they comfort me. (Psalm 23:4, ESV)*

I face an older person's danger today. I have a strong tendency to make the past sound better than it really was. "Good old days" syndrome!

An honest appraisal shows us that some things were better in the past and some things were worse. One of the things that was better was a greater safety in our streets for kids.

I was a 13-year-old paperboy, getting up at 3:30 a.m. every morning to fold and pack my papers and put them on my bicycle. Off into the dark by 4 a.m., I typically finished by 5-5:30 and could crawl back into bed for a short finish to the night's sleep. It would never be allowed today, and yet my loving parents never considered it to be dangerous. Different times.

I had a large area for my route and most of it was in our lower-middle-class neighborhood. A few streets though, led me through some pretty run-down areas. To put it bluntly, today I wouldn't want to drive through the area in my car, much less send a teenager through it at night on a bike. Most of the time, I was oblivious to the possibility of danger. But occasionally a few things happened to bring fear to the surface. Nothing major, more like "things that go bump in the night," but nonetheless, it created some fear in this 13-year-old paperboy.

How do you handle fear in dark places? In our youth group at church, we had been learning a new chorus based on the 23rd Psalm. It was a simple melody, often sung as a round, and it stuck in my mind.

The Lord Is My Shepherd
I'll Walk with Him Always
The Lord is my Shepherd
I'll walk with Him always;
He leads me beside still waters
I'll walk with Him always.
Always, always
I'll walk with Him always;
Always, always
I'll walk with Him always.

—Composer Unknown

God used it to bring peace to me on some of those dark mornings. I would ever so softly begin to sing that simple chorus as I pedaled my bike through the rough areas. As I focused on the one who walked with me, even through dark places, I realized that I did not need to fear any evil. Peace replaced fear because of the awareness of the presence of Christ with me.

I almost didn't use the 23rd Psalm as a text today because it doesn't actually have the word "peace" in it. Yet the entire psalm is about peace. From green pastures and still waters to dwelling forever in his house, David gives us a picture of peace and the means of peace. The key to all of what the psalm promises is the presence of God. "Though I walk through the valley of the shadow of death, I will not fear, because you are with me."

For followers of Jesus, the indwelling Spirit is an absolute promise. He *is* with us! The trouble often is our lack of awareness of that fact in the moment of danger or fear. That's why it is so important to bring the power of the Word of God into our lives continually. Somehow as a 13-year-old paperboy, I stumbled onto a truth that has served me well for many years. Whether it is singing a psalm or praying it without melody, the promises of his presence will bring peace.

My Prayer

Lord, I am so grateful that you have provided for me green pastures to lay down in and still water to walk alongside. Thank you for preparing a table before me, even in the presence of my enemies. How grateful to know that your goodness and mercy will be with me always and that you have provided for me an eternal home. Most of all Lord, I am grateful that your presence is continually with me. Keep me aware of that amazing fact. Thank you for the peace that comes from your presence.

Prayer Point

Make it a point each day to affirm the Lord's presence in your life. You can use the phrase from Psalm 23 and simply say . . . "because you are with me."

DAY 6

Blessed with Peace

The LORD gives strength to his people; the LORD blesses his people with peace. (Psalm 29:11)

Have you been blessed by the Lord's peace? Given the trials and difficulties we all go through, how wonderful to know that God wants to give us his peace. Of course, like almost everything else that the Lord wants to give us, we must ask. My friend, Sue, shared this story of a time she needed and asked for peace.

My husband and I were going thru some medical concerns with him and we needed to travel a distance for a special test. He normally does most of the driving, but since he was recovering from a recent surgery, that responsibility fell to me. As I looked over to him in the seat next to me, dozing peacefully, I came to the realization that I was NOT peaceful! I had chest tightness and my mind was racing. Ok God, my prayer began, I need you now, right this minute, I need the peace that only you can bring. I need peace for driving right now. I need peace for our journey ahead with my husband's health. I need peace for my strength in the coming months. I didn't hear any "voice" from the heaven, but about five miles down the road, I noticed my chest tightness had eased considerably and I truly felt "peaceful"! God came to me very peacefully, just like I needed (and asked) for him.

It's a simple story with a simple need, but that's where most of us are in our lives. We face situations that bring stress and uncertainty on a regular basis. Even the very environment in which we live and work often breeds low-grade stress and anxiety. The great need of our life is peace. The good news is we worship a God who wants to bless us with peace!

So why then, do so many Christians go about in anxiety and worry, lacking the peace they so desperately need? At least one major reason is a failure to ask. James tell us, "You do not have because you do not ask God" (James 4:2). How often are you asking for peace? And if you do ask, do you believe that God truly wants to give you his peace?

That's why I love the Word of God that gives us insight into what God desires to do in relationship to his people. The psalmist clearly tells us that God desires to bless his people with peace. When we ask for peace, we are not trying to talk a reluctant God into giving us something that we're not sure he wants to give us. God wants to bless us with his peace. That gives us freedom and boldness to ask in complete faith for the peace needed to give us strength for each day.

My Prayer

Father, you know the great need I have for your peace in my life. There are so many things that come along daily that seem to sap my strength and bring worry. I'm so grateful for your Word that assures me of your desire to bless me with your peace. Because of that, today I come before you with confidence, asking for the blessing of peace in my life.

Prayer Point

Scripture is so clear that we do not have because we do not ask. Ask the Lord today to bless your life with his peace.

DAY 7

The God of Peace

For God is not a God of confusion but of peace. (1 Corinthians 14:33, ESV)

Paul wrote this oft-quoted verse to deal with issues within a local church body, but the principle is true for individual situations as well. God does not want us to walk in the stress and anxiety of confusion but in the peace that comes from his presence in our lives.

That truth hit home for my wife Kim and me a number of years ago as we were discussing his lifework with our youngest son, David.

Since childhood, David desired to be a policeman. We never seriously considered that, assuming he would outgrow it. After all, he also wanted to be an ice-cream truck driver, and he did outgrow that. But the desire for police work never left him and it began to be a point of contention with us. Tension often marked our discussions. You can imagine we were very worried about the dangers he would face on a regular basis as a law enforcement officer.

We kept presenting other options for a career, but it always came back to law enforcement for David. We had no peace about this and felt great confusion. We spent significant time praying for God to change David's heart . . . or to change ours. God gave us his answer one day when our son sat us down and said, "I believe God has called me into law enforcement as my ministry." He went on to describe for us how he believed he could be used by God to change lives through a career as a policeman.

It was astonishing how fast God cut through the confusion in our lives and brought almost immediate peace. The Lord was at work in our son's life and he had him in the palm of his hand. There was a call of God to ministry that was now undeniable, and we accepted that with the peace that God provided.

God doesn't want his children wandering about in confusion, but walking in his ways in the peace he provides. The interesting thing that God taught us in this circumstance is that God's peace doesn't always bend to our desires. The peace of God doesn't come when God lines up circumstances to match what we want. It is exactly the opposite. We experience his peace when we begin to line up with his will and purpose. Confusion comes when my self-will gets in the way. Peace comes when God has his way.

My Prayer

Father, I thank you that you do not create confusion. As you brought order out of chaos at the creation of all things, so you desire to bring order out of the chaos of my life. Thank you for being a God of peace. Help me to so order my desires and life that I always match up to your peace.

Prayer Point

We all face choices that can create confusion. Ask the Lord to replace confusion with his peace.

DAY 8

Peace Amid the Flood

*Grace, mercy and peace from God the Father and from Jesus
Christ, the Father's Son, will be with us in truth and love. (2
John 1:3)*

God is so committed to us experiencing his grace, mercy and
peace that sometimes he goes to extraordinary lengths to
communicate that to us. That's what happened to my friends
Don and Annora Null in the midst of a devastating flood. Here's their
story from Annora's perspective:

It was in June of 2008 but I remember it well. We had gone to the
first night of Don's 50th high school class reunion at the Gerstmeyer
Tech gym. It was raining really hard when we left to come home.
It rained all night and about 5:30 a.m. or so, our chihuahua woke
me up whining. I got up to comfort her and saw how much water
was standing in our yard. When I went to the front of the house
and turned on the porch light, the water had already risen to the
level of our porch. I awoke Don and he immediately started to
assess the situation. Christina, our daughter, and Devinn, her
son, were living with us at the time as well as her black lab mix
dog and our other daughter's black lab, so we woke them up also
to start putting things up off the floors and onto countertops and
beds, etc. etc. The lower parts of closets and shelving were soon
to be in jeopardy. . . .

Meanwhile I sat down at the table and called a man that I knew
from my real estate career who did restoration. He had no idea
what was happening in our end of town but said he would come
by later that day. Then I heard God say to me—not in an audible
voice—but I heard or felt or experienced God's words to me. He

said "Am I enough for you?" I said, "Yes, Lord, you are enough." Then He repeated, "Am I enough for you?" Again I responded, "Yes, Lord, you are enough for me." Three times, He asked the same question and three times, I affirmed that He was enough for me. It was then that God's peace took over.

I cannot say the next five or six months were easy, but I knew we would make it one way or another. Don and I encouraged one another as we recovered and through all the meetings with FEMA, Salvation Army, flood insurance adjusters, etc. As a result of the flood, our house was stripped down to the studs and restored better than it had been before the flood. God promised to never leave us nor forsake us, didn't he? His presence brought peace through the flood.

Run a search of the word "peace" in Scriptures and you will find hundreds of occurrences of the word. Even more telling is Jesus' use of the word, both in greeting and in teaching. God wants his people to experience peace. I'm convinced the reason for this emphasis is that peace is directly tied to the presence of God. In the presence of the Lord, we will know peace.

In many ways, the whole gospel message is about the presence of God showing up in the midst of human life. When the angels appeared to the shepherds at the birth of Jesus, they announced peace to people because God had showed up. True peace with God and with one another is now possible because Emmanuel, the God who is with us, has now come.

Peace then, is one of the key indicators of the presence of God in our lives. It is no wonder that it is emphasized so much in the Word. When we draw near to the Lord and seek his presence, we begin to experience his peace. God's great desire is that we seek him, find him, and that he would come to dwell in us through his spirit. Peace is the great marker of that, along with joy.

My Prayer

Lord, I am so grateful for your presence in my life through your spirit, filling me with your grace, mercy, and peace. May your peace pervade every aspect of my life, demonstrating to all around me of your amazing presence. Lord, regardless of what happens around me, I confess, You are enough!

Prayer Point

As you are worshiping or praying, ask the Lord to allow you to experience the peace of his presence in a very special way.

DAY 9

Peace and Your Comfort Zone

Again Jesus said, "Peace be with you! As the Father has sent me, I am sending you." (John 20:21)

Jesus often puts words together that don't seem to fit, like "peace" and "sending you." Rarely does being sent somewhere imply peace. It's usually a mission that takes us out of our comfort zone, and that typically takes away peace instead of giving it. But Jesus puts the two together because ultimately, our real comfort zone is wherever the Lord is sending us.

When Kim and I were sensing God's call for us to leave a local pastorate and begin a prayer ministry, we had that struggle between being sent and leaving our comfort zone. To gauge how this effort might be received, I called five friends who were national Christian leaders and told them of our desire. In a fascinating way, all five of these men said exactly the same thing. They told us three things:

1. There is a great need.
2. You're the ones to do this.
3. We think you'll starve.

They just didn't see how we could find the financial support for a full-time prayer ministry. Talk about something that steals your peace.

We pursued some other ways of doing prayer ministry part-time for about nine months. One day, while in a paddleboat on a beautiful, quiet, tree-lined lake, God met us in a special way. He reaffirmed his call to us. In that place of peace, his wonderful peace was poured out upon us and Harvest Prayer Ministries was born. We still had no financial support. The outward circumstances had not changed. But his peace was spoken over us and his sending was affirmed.

Where is God sending you? Yes, he is sending you. It may not be across the world, or to start a new ministry, but followers of Jesus are "sent ones." It may be to a particular family in your neighborhood or community, but he is sending you. The main question is whether or not you are going. Sending is always an issue of change. It is often accompanied by anxiety or fear. But peace is offered if we will go.

When Jesus spoke of both peace and sending to his disciples in John 20:21, he tied that to the fact the he himself had been sent by the Father. Jesus accepted being sent by the Father and he walked in amazing peace. Now as he was sending his disciples, he gave them the same promise of peace. Our job is to draw near to him in prayer and experience the peace of his presence.

My Prayer

Lord Jesus, thank you for being willing to be sent by the Father for our benefit. Now Lord, help me to accept your call to go wherever you would send me. With the promise of your presence and your peace, I am able to go and do whatever you ask. I draw near to you now and with your peace covering me, I am content.

Prayer Point

Is there a challenge ahead of you that might take you out of your comfort zone? Ask for the peace of his presence to assure you of his calling.

Peace that Passes Understanding

And the peace of God, which transcends all understanding, will guard your hearts and your minds in Christ Jesus. (Philippians 4:7)

The Lord has amazing timing, doesn't he? For several months, I have been pulling together resources and studying Scriptures to write this devotional. By the time I sat down to actually write it, peace had become far more than just a topic to study. It was becoming an integral part of my life. I had no idea how important that was to become.

I often withdraw to other places to write, and I did so for this devotional. The Holy Spirit was at work and it seemed like the devotionals flowed for several days. Then came the call. It was a call I was waiting for from some medical tests I had done a week earlier. The tests results showed that I had a rare form of cancer called B Cell Mantle Lymphoma. I confess that the writing stopped for two days while my wife, Kim, and I scoured the internet to learn all we could of this disease. As we learned, we discovered things we didn't want to know! This was going to be a full-on struggle to survive! I can honestly say that though we had moments of uncertainty and stress, God's peace never left us.

Writing a manuscript on God's peace in an imperfect world was a miraculous blessing from God to prepare me through his Word, with his peace, for the news he knew I would soon receive. Far more than just an academic topic, his peace is a reality. A precious gift to be received and for which we give thanks.

It is a peace beyond understanding. A cancer diagnosis typically brings much fear and anxiety and I do not pretend that there have not been anxious thoughts. But in a way I do not understand and cannot begin to explain, God's amazing peace has guarded our hearts and minds through Christ Jesus.

I think the key word is guard. It isn't that there are not anxious thoughts and fears that arise. But a guard has supernaturally been set upon our hearts through Christ Jesus. This guard is awake and alert and prevents the natural thoughts and fears from gaining a foothold in our lives. Our minds and emotions do not have to be subservient to the circumstances around us. The peace of God is a strong guard that protects us and allows us to overcome a situation with the thoughts that come from him.

Once again, the key to all of this is desiring it and asking for it. You can read Philippians 4:7 and feel good about it but if you do not, through prayer and faith, accept it into your life, it is simply nice words. God's peace is available for all followers of Christ if we will ask for it and accept it into our lives. Then we can cultivate his peace through a life of prayer and trust.

My Prayer

How grateful I am Lord, for your timing and the way you prepared me for the news of the medical issues I face. But you had already placed your peace in my life to guard and protect me. I know Lord, you want this for all your people. Help us to be those who walk daily in your peace as we spend our days with you.

Prayer Point

Ask the Lord to place peace as a guard for your heart and mind.

Peace and the Gospel

He came and preached peace to you who were far away and peace to those who were near. (Ephesians 2:17)

Jesus preached the gospel of peace and those who responded received His peace. That wasn't just a first century phenomenon but has been the case through the centuries. The great English preacher and revivalist John Wesley experienced people responding to his preaching by receiving the peace of Christ.

To Wesley's surprise, he began to experience the Holy Spirit powerfully convicting people of sins while he preached. Well-dressed, mature people suddenly cried out as if in the agonies of death. Both men and women, outside and inside the church buildings, would tremble and sink to the ground. When Wesley stopped and prayed for them, they soon found PEACE and rejoiced in Christ.—Wesley Duewel, *Revival Fire,* p.77

This is the proper sequence:
1. Hearing the truth of the gospel
2. Conviction of sin through the work of the Holy Spirit
3. Peace through the acceptance of and obedience to the gospel.

If you feel far apart from Jesus and struggle to find peace in your life, could I suggest you begin at the beginning?

I'm not in any way trying to get believers to doubt their salvation, but sometimes you need to go over the basics to affirm where you are in Christ.
1. Do you know the gospel?
2. Have you experienced the conviction of the Holy Spirit and repented of your sins?

3. Have you affirmed Christ as Lord of your life and committed to follow him in all that he says?

Spend some time praying over this and as you affirm each of these, watch as the peace of Christ begins to change your emotions and thoughts.

Whether you have been following Christ for years or are just coming to faith, listen to how the Apostle Paul sums up the gospel.

Now, brothers and sisters, I want to remind you of the gospel I preached to you, which you received and on which you have taken your stand. By this gospel you are saved, if you hold firmly to the word I preached to you. Otherwise, you have believed in vain. For what I received I passed on to you as of first importance: that Christ died for our sins according to the Scriptures, that he was buried, that he was raised on the third day according to the Scriptures, and that he appeared to Cephas, and then to the Twelve. (1 Corinthians 15:1-5)

This is the gospel of peace that Jesus preached to both Jews and Gentiles. It is still being preached to each of us today. Walking in the truth of the gospel means walking in the peace of Christ. It is a big part of what it means to live the Christian life. We should have a firm expectation of his peace guarding our hearts each day.

My Prayer

Lord Jesus, thank you for preaching the gospel of peace. You knew how much we would need that in our lives. You have provided for us through your life, death, burial, and resurrection all that we need for peace in this world and forever in your eternal house. Forgive me when I forget what you have provided and wallow in anxiety and fear. Today, I choose the peace that comes from your presence in my life.

Prayer Point

Spend time today praying over the gospel. Thank the Lord for what he has done for you and accept his peace fully into your life.

Be Found at Peace

So then, dear friends, since you are looking forward to this, make every effort to be found spotless, blameless and at peace with him. (2 Peter 3:14)

I'm convinced that one of the distinguishing marks of the End-Times Church will be peace. In Peter's second epistle he speaks of those who scoff at biblical prophecy regarding the Lord's return. Then Peter moves into a harrowing description of what will happen: "But the day of the Lord will come like a thief. The heavens will disappear with a roar; the elements will be destroyed by fire, and the earth and everything done in it will be laid bare" (2 Peter 3:10).

These are all things that should bring great fear to those who read and believe. Yet followers of Jesus should be those who actually "look forward to the day of God" and live in peace even in the midst of chaos and confusion. It is a peace that Jesus provides for us that is not based on circumstances around us or even feelings within us. It is a peace that comes from his presence in our lives. It is a peace that allows us to walk through even extremely difficult circumstances because he is with us.

I remember my dad telling me how the troop ship he was in during World War 2, while on its way to England in a convoy, was attacked by German U-boats. Obviously there was not a thing that soldiers on a troop ship could do to defend against submarine attack. So Dad and some of his friends did the only thing they knew to do . . . they prayed. Down in the bunk rooms of the ship, they gathered on the bunks to pray and ask God's protection. Dad said that was the only sense of peace they felt on the whole trip. Not a ship was lost and they made it safely to England.

Your fears may not be about the end-times, and likely do not deal with submarine attacks, but we all face fear and anxiety of some sort. It may be relationships in your family, it might be financial problems, or even generalized anxiety over life itself. I want you to know that Jesus is willing and ready to walk with you through your shadows and bring you to his light in peace. It doesn't always mean that your circumstances change, but it does mean you face them from a whole different perspective. It's the peaceful presence of Christ that makes all the difference.

My Prayer

Lord, I am so grateful for your presence that brings peace. It is so easy for me to fall back into my own fears, insecurities and anxieties, while all along you were there, waiting for me to turn to you. Forgive me for forgetting your readiness and love. I turn to you now for the peace that I desperately need in my walk through this world.

Prayer Point

Remind yourself today that Jesus is waiting and willing to give you his peace as he walks with you through the day. Perhaps find a scripture regarding his peace that you could tape to the mirror in the morning. Memorize it, and then call it to mind throughout the day.

DAY 13

Peace, a Fruit of the Spirit

But the fruit of the Spirit is love, joy, peace, forbearance, kindness, goodness, faithfulness. (Galatians 5:22)

The fact that peace is a fruit of the Spirit is simply biblical truth. It can become for us a matter-of-fact, intellectual truth that doesn't impact us until we see it up close and personal.

The week I was working on this devotional, I received a blog from a former teacher and friend, Dr. Eleanor Daniel regarding the work of peace in her life. I share it here. Two days after she wrote this blog, she went home to Jesus.

Today's post has particularly personal meeting. It's my 77th birthday, celebrated with great joy with my four siblings and other family and friends. But even more significantly, when we began drafting this post a couple of weeks ago, we could talk about PEACE as a fruit of the spirit in academic terms. I have found that peace is a very personal matter right now. Life is undergoing a big change. I have been on dialysis for over three years and had anticipated being on it for some time more. That is not to be. In the progression of things it is important to stop dialysis. My final dialysis treatment was this past Friday. And I can anticipate a couple of weeks to live. When I returned from the hospital three days ago, I shared the fact that I am no longer on dialysis with one of my close friends in the nursing home. She said to me, "You look different. You look well! You're at peace, aren't you." I AM AT PEACE—the peace that passes understanding.

And now, "The Lord bless you and keep you. The Lord make his face to shine upon you and be gracious unto you. The Lord turn his face toward you and give you PEACE" (Numbers 6:24-26, emphasis added). —Dr. Eleanor Daniel

When peace as a fruit of the Spirit has been cultivated and is allowed to grow in our lives, it allows us to deal with absolutely anything that comes our way. Cultivating peace means standing against that which is not peace. When anxiety rears its head, we reject it rather than embrace it. The worries that often come our way are rejected. When we are plagued by "what if?" thoughts, we turn from that, recognizing it as unprofitable thinking. Most of all, we continually come before Jesus in prayer, asking him to grant us his peace.

The fruit of the Spirit that is peace is not about the absence of violence or merely a passive acceptance of things as they are. This peace is never about changing our outward circumstances to make life easy for us. It is always about walking close to the Prince of Peace and allowing him to deal with everything we are facing. In his presence, we dwell in peace. It becomes a permanent way of life.

My Prayer

Thank you Lord, for giving me your Spirit and allowing the fruit of your Spirit's presence to be growing and active in my life. I know Lord, that each of those qualities or characteristics must be cared for and desired. I especially today take the peace you have given me through your Spirit and ask you to cause that to grow to the point where your peace overcomes everything that might attempt to steal that peace.

Prayer Point

Like virtually everything in the Kingdom of God, peace must be sought and asked for. Would you make the pursuit of the peace of Christ a part of your everyday prayer time?

DAY 14

Seek Peace

Turn from evil and do good; seek peace and pursue it. (Psalm 34:14)

As I write today's devotional, I am in the midst of an intensive chemotherapy treatment to deal with my aggressive cancer. I can't imagine anything more designed to steal peace than chemo. It doesn't just affect the body with harmful side-effects, it also creates a whole new way of life for the patient. My lowered immune system means I stay away from people unless I know they don't have any sickness. There's a steep learning curve for what foods I can and cannot eat. I walk around my house disinfecting anything and everything to avoid the risk of secondary infections. All of these very necessary things can create fear rather than peace.

In a situation like this, I've learned how practical Scripture is regarding peace. It doesn't just happen. Though it is a gift of God, it is to be asked for, received, cultivated, and pursued. All too often in the Christian life, we can fall into an unhealthy passivity. It sounds spiritual to say something like, "let go and let God," but that's rarely how we grow spiritually. The Apostle Paul presents an active spirituality that is "pressing forward," not kicking back and relaxing.

I know that for me personally, pursuing peace during chemotherapy has meant looking for Scripture passages that teach me more of what the peace of God is. It has meant actively praying those scriptures regarding peace into my life on a daily basis, asking Jesus Christ to bring those things to pass within me. It has also meant listening to the testimony of other believers who have sought and found the peace of God.

Without a doubt, the most powerful thing I have learned regarding pursuing peace is that it means pursuing the presence of Christ. Again and again I have found myself waking through the night with a passion to get up and worship the Lord. Seeking his face has meant walking in his peace. As I have delighted myself in his presence, fear always leaves and is replaced by the peace that is beyond understanding. And it is not just through the night hours. Worship throughout the day has become a way of life as I pursue peace.

My Prayer

Lord, I delight in the fact that you both give us peace and at the same time ask us to pursue it. We all run after those things that are important to us. Your peace is so vital to our lives and well-being. I draw near to you today, enjoying your presence and accepting the peace you so freely offer.

Prayer Point

Determine today how you will pursue peace. Bring that to Jesus in prayer and ask him to bless your pursuit.

DAY 15
Let Your Peace Come

If the home is deserving, let your peace rest on it; if it is not, let your peace return to you. (Matthew 10:13)

Ok, admit it. This is one of those weird verses that we tend to gloss over and not really deal with. Jesus treats peace here as almost a physical commodity to be given and taken away. That's just not the way we normally look at peace. But since it's Jesus saying it, we'd better pay close attention. He always gets it right.

Jesus had peace within him. He could not only speak of peace, but could offer it to others. And in a wonderful transference, he gave that ability to his followers. When the peace of Christ becomes a living reality within us, we not only speak of it, but we offer it to others. In practical ways that means we pray God's peace for others, we model living in peace in front of others, and we offer the good news of the Prince of Peace to those who do not know him. When we do this, we become distributors of the peace of God!

One very practical and historical way of doing this, and of regularly reminding ourselves that we can indeed give peace, is the "passing of peace" during a worship service. I did not grow up in a church tradition where this was practiced, but I find it to be a helpful way of speaking peace into others' lives and receiving peace from others.

The following excerpt was found online and it gives some insight into this ancient and modern practice.

Christian worship is filled with profound actions: heads bowed in prayer, arms raised in praise, standing in reverence during a Scripture reading, coming forward to give an offering. One ancient and significant gesture in worship is the passing of the peace. Passing the peace is a tradition rooted in Scripture that embodies our identity as peacemakers (Matt. 5:9; 2 Cor. 5:20) and trains ours hearts, hands, and tongues in the ways of peace.

From the beginning Christians have exercised this practice. "Peace be with you" is a greeting Jesus himself used with his disciples (Luke 24:36; John 20:19, 26). The apostle Paul opened each of his letters with the words "Grace and peace be with you" (Rom. 1:7; 1 Cor. 1:3; 2 Cor. 1:2).

Today in many congregations, we may pass the peace during a mutual greeting, after words of assurance, prior to celebrating the Lord's Supper, or at the conclusion of a worship service. At these times we leave the comfort of our seat, turn to our neighbors, grasp their hands, and speak the words, "The peace of the Lord be with you" and receive the words in turn, "And also with you."

The gesture is simple, but the meaning is profound. When we extend our hand to another, we identify with Jesus, who extended his life to the point of death to make peace with humanity (Col. 1:20-21). What's more, in the midst of divisions, we symbolize our unity through handshakes and hugs (Eph. 2:14-21). Likewise, when we regularly pass the peace, we practice God's call to make every effort to maintain the bond of peace (Eph. 4:3). —from *ReformedWorship.org*, Issue 99, March 2011

Whether you choose to "pass the peace" in worship gatherings or not, we all need to accept our role as those who are emissaries of the Prince of Peace. We live out his peace in our lives. We look for ways to give his peace to others. We learn to shout with the angels outside of Bethlehem long ago, "on earth peace, good will toward men" (Luke 2:14).

My Prayer

Lord, thank you for giving me your peace. You literally spoke it into being in my life and I am so grateful. Help me to carry your peace with me wherever I go. Forgive me when I have failed and instead brought division and dissension. Show me how I can give your peace to those around me today.

Prayer Point

Choose today to whom you will give the peace of Christ. Ask the Lord to open the door for you to do so.

DAY 16

Things That Make for Peace

"If you, even you, had only known on this day what would bring you peace—but now it is hidden from your eyes." (Luke 19:42)

It is so easy to miss out on peace. We get so caught up in circumstances and emotions that we forget to stay attached to Jesus and to enjoy the peace that comes from his presence. That, of course, happens to us as individuals all the time, I'm afraid. But it can also happen to a group of people or even a nation. When Jesus came to Jerusalem during what we call his triumphal entry, he commented that peace was hidden from the city because they just didn't understand who was coming into their midst, carrying peace with him.

That day long ago could have changed the history of the Jewish people and the city of Jerusalem forever. But they missed seeing peace that day. It was hidden from their eyes, according to Jesus. Instead of peace, within a generation Jerusalem was destroyed and the Jewish people dispersed around the world. Missing peace has grave consequences. It still does!

Recently, a good friend called me to tell me about his experience sitting on a jury for a murder trial. One of the things he learned was that at the conclusion of the charges against the accused was the phrase, "he acted against the peace and dignity of the state." It turns out that this is the required phrase at the end of virtually all charges. This phrase is derived from the Latin phrase, *contra pacem domini regis,* which means "against the peace of the Lord the King." In ancient times, it was used in indictments and civil actions of trespass. Even in courts of law in our nation, peace in the land is recognized as being so precious that to disturb or take away peace becomes a serious charge.

I'm convinced that when civil unrest breaks out in a nation, it is almost always a result of a failure to recognize the presence of Christ, who brings peace to the soul, and which then begins to filter into the culture. In the United States, as we have increasingly moved toward becoming a secular society, we can expect more and more unrest and violence, as the peace of Christ is held in less and less esteem and desire. As Jesus would say, "the things that make for peace are hidden from your eyes."

You might feel powerless to stop such a powerful secular move in our society, but there's one thing you and I can do. We can make sure peace is not hidden from us. We can and should embrace the peace that comes from the presence of Christ. Christ followers should be known as a people of peace, both within themselves and outwardly as we interact with those around us. When millions of Christians walk through life in the peace of Christ, a culture and society can be changed.

My Prayer

Prince of Peace, how I desire you in my life and in our nation. I recognize the desperate need for your peace, a peace that comes from my relationship with you. Pour that out upon all your people, please. Give us the boldness to speak and live peace wherever we might be. May your peace begin to bring transformation to our nation as you increasingly are recognized as Lord!

Prayer Point

Pray especially for peace in our nation that comes through acknowledgment of who Christ is.

DAY 17

Let Peace Rule

Let the peace of Christ rule in your hearts, since as members of one
body you were called to peace. And be thankful. (Colossians 3:15)

When speaking of peace in Colossians, Paul pulls out all the stops and hits us with the word "rule." Peace is to rule in our hearts. This is a far cry from an emotion of peacefulness or an attitude we have somehow developed. Ruling is a powerful word that indicates the ability to transform and direct the activities of your life. The peace of Christ has that innate ability to rule.

It is interesting that Paul's command is that we let peace do its ruling work in our hearts. The peace of Christ, let loose in your life, will rule and direct you in ways that line up with the purposes of Christ. Our job is to let that happen. In a sense, that means that we give permission to the peace of Christ to rule. You get to choose who or what will rule in your heart. God's Word tells us that the very best thing we can do is let peace take over.

Sometimes it seems that life throws everything it has got at you, all at once. In the fall of 1998 that happened to Kim and me. My father was in the last stages of his five-year battle with lymphoma. My mother, who was his primary caregiver, suffered a massive stroke that paralyzed her right side for the rest of her life. Dad was on one floor of the hospital and Mom on another. My mom's brother was on yet another floor of the hospital, dying from cancer. In the midst of that, we got a call that Kim's mom had a TIA (Transient Ischemic Attack—a mini-stroke that dissolves on its own) giving us the fear of another stroke coming in the family.

We ran into the arms of Jesus. There was nowhere else to go. His peace enveloped us and though circumstances did not change, I can say with confidence that his peace began to rule in our hearts.

45

The peace of Christ was in charge, not the circumstances of failing health and fear.

The key is our choice. Regardless of what is happening in or around us that is stealing our peace or creating anxiety, we can still choose to let peace rule in our hearts. This is where faith steps in and takes over. We go to God's Word which tells us to simply let the peace of Christ rule in our hearts, and though that seems woefully inadequate in the face of our fears, we, by faith, say yes to the Word of God. We pray that truth into our lives and watch and see what God does with an obedient, faithful heart.

My Prayer

Lord, today I choose to let your peace rule in my heart. Regardless of what happens around me, it is your peace that will rule within. Thank you that we have literally been called to this peace by you. I am grateful!

Prayer Point

Memorize Colossians 3:15. Begin each day by affirming that the peace of Christ is ruling in your heart.

DAY 18

Peace Be Still!

That day when evening came, he said to his disciples, "Let us go over to the other side." Leaving the crowd behind, they took him along, just as he was, in the boat. There were also other boats with him. A furious squall came up, and the waves broke over the boat, so that it was nearly swamped. Jesus was in the stern, sleeping on a cushion. The disciples woke him and said to him, "Teacher, don't you care if we drown?" He got up, rebuked the wind and said to the waves, "Quiet! Be still!" Then the wind died down and it was completely calm. He said to his disciples, "Why are you so afraid? Do you still have no faith?" They were terrified and asked each other, "Who is this? Even the wind and the waves obey him!" (Mark 4:35-41)

Several times, I have had the privilege of being on the Sea of Galilee, where this event took place. But they were all times of calm weather. I've not endured one of the quick, violent storms for which this lake is known. But having seen the hills surrounding this small body of water, I understand how conditions can quickly change with the wind whipping down the hills onto the water. Even experienced sailors can find themselves in trouble on the sea. That's what happened to Jesus and the disciples in this compelling story of faith, peace, and power.

As the storm hit and the waves began breaking into the boat, everyone was filled with fear. Everyone except Jesus. He was asleep in the stern of the boat. Finally, the fear got the best of the disciples and they woke Jesus with the whining and illogical question, "Teacher, don't you care if we drown?" Ignoring that question, Jesus got up and spoke peace to the wind and the sea. Doing what only the power of God could do, the wind and waves ceased and everything became calm. Everything was calm except for the disciples. They were still worked up emotionally by what had happened.

Jesus realized the fear that was governing the disciples and moved into a powerful time of teaching, both for them and for us. As he so often did, he moved into teaching mode by asking questions: Why are you so afraid? Have you still no faith? I certainly understand the fear of the disciples. At the heart of it is the fear of dying. These were experienced fishermen who knew they were in danger of losing their lives in this storm. That caused them to wake Jesus and ask the man they knew cared more than anyone they'd ever met, if he cared whether they were perishing. Fear often pushes us into irrational words and actions.

What storm are you facing today? Is it a serious illness for you or someone you love? Are you facing serious debt or financial crisis? Maybe the storm has to do with your children or grandchildren and issues that seem to have no easy answers. The list could go on, couldn't it? Unfortunately, like the disciples on the Sea of Galilee, these storms often cause us to react in ways that don't solve the problem, but often make it even worse. What we really want is for Jesus to speak to the storm and calm it.

The trouble is, that doesn't always remove the fear. At least it didn't for the disciples. That's why Jesus asked the second question: Have you still no faith? They had, with their own eyes, watched Jesus stop the wind and calm the waves. It was an astonishing miracle. But still they had fear. I think that we need to pay close attention to this incident, but often, we have so allowed fear to take root in our lives, that even a miracle from the Lord will not cause the fear to subside.

Jesus connected their fear to a lack of faith. The heart of this issue is, who is in your boat? They certainly had experienced a miracle from Jesus, but their lack of understanding of who Jesus was caused them still to fear. After the miracle, and after the questions from Jesus, Scripture says, "They were terrified and asked each other, 'Who is this? Even the wind and the waves obey him!'" They still had no idea who was in the boat with them. Had they understood that God was in their boat, there would have been no fear. Lack of faith in who Jesus is creates fear, even in those who love him.

Who is in your boat? When contemporary storms are rocking your world, have you looked over at the sleeping figure in your boat and said, "God is in my boat!"

Spending time with Jesus in prayer develops an awareness of his presence, even in the midst of tough times. You will see him in every circumstance. This lifestyle of cultivating his presence allows you to know that when God is in your boat, there's no room for fear.

My Prayer

Lord, help me to know you as Creator God, King of Kings and Lord of Lords. You are the one who has promised to be with me always. You are in my boat in the midst of any and every storm. May the peace of your presence allow me to trust you and turn from all fear.

Prayer Point

Daily cultivate an awareness of the presence of Jesus in your life that goes way beyond a devotional time or small segment of your day. Continue to pray for Jesus' presence in all aspects of your life.

DAY 19

Come in Peace

"So that I come again to my father's house in peace, then the LORD *shall be my God." (Genesis 28:21, ESV)*

The sons of Isaac, Jacob and Esau, often created situations that led to turmoil, both in their family and in their own lives. Deception, selfishness, lack of spiritual growth, and spiritual laziness often set brother against brother and drew their parents into places of conflict and confusion. Peace was not a big part of this family!

After Jacob's amazing encounter with God at Bethel, his heart began to change. He sought peace with his family and his God. Even though it was going to be a long-term process, peace in Jacob's life was now a priority for him.

That's one of the key results of coming face-to-face with God. Walking in God's presence daily is the essence of what we call revival. Revival that revolves around the presence of God produces peace!

Has peace been elusive for you? Whether in your family, your workplace, or in your own emotional life, is peace a missing element? So many struggle to find peace and yet find that it escapes them. Look at what happened with Jacob. He was far from a man of peace until he encountered God. The God of peace brings peace with him. When you seek him and encounter him, his peace begins to flood into your life. A life of continual seeking after the Lord brings a life of peace.

Peace is found in the Father's lap. A funny story from my childhood illustrates that. I was just a little boy at a family reunion. I was walking along the edge of the house of the family we were visiting. At the corner, I walked right into the big, old family dog. He was bigger than I was and startled me. I began to run. Now I'm sure the dog was thinking that this boy was ready to play, so it came running after me. Which terrified me all the more. The only safe place I could think of was

50

where my father was sitting in the front yard, full of relatives sitting in the shade. I hit the front yard running as fast as I could run with the dog at my heels. I saw my dad in his chair and launched myself in the air, landing right on his lap. The length of the leap might have grown with the telling through the years, but all I knew was that the only place of safety and peace was my father's lap.

That's true for our heavenly Father's lap as well. We draw near to him and he draws near to us (see James 4:8). In his presence is peace. It is a peace that not only transforms our own lives, but also impacts those around us. We say with Jacob, "I come again to my father's house in peace."

My Prayer

Father, I come to you, the source of all peace. Your house is a place of peace and I come at your invitation to dwell in your house all the days of my life. Teach me to draw near each day, that your peace would pervade every aspect of my life.

Prayer Point

Since peace is found in the Father's house, it is essential for you to draw near daily and confess your need to dwell in God's house.

You May Have Peace

"I have said these things to you, that in me you may have peace. In the world you will have tribulation. But take heart; I have overcome the world." (John 16:33, ESV)

Jesus makes two very serious promises that believers of all generations must comprehend if they are to live in accordance with the words of Jesus. First of all, Jesus promises that in him we may have peace. Secondly, he promises us that in the world you will have tribulation. Talk about contrasting promises! Peace and tribulation don't go together at all in our ordinary way of looking at situations. But Jesus knows how things fit together far better than any of us and we must heed his words.

Looking at the first promise causes us to see that Jesus lived what he promised. In his short 33 years in the flesh on earth, he was surrounded by turmoil and controversy that typically take away peace. Yet, he lived his years here modeling peace. He often was the only one who seemed to be under self-control in any situation. Especially during his arrest and trial, the Prince of Peace demonstrated what it meant to live out peace in the midst of chaos.

The promise of Jesus is that this kind of peace is what we can have. It is because that peace is in him and when believers choose to live in him, his peace becomes possible for us. If you are a Christian and not experiencing his peace, then I want to point out to you the exactness with which Jesus gives this promise. Jesus said, "in me you *may* have peace." You have to desire this peace, ask for it in prayer, and commit to live it out.

The second, contrasting promise is what we are much more aware of in our lives. In this world, you will have tribulation. This is not an end-time remark about the Great Tribulation. It is a clear declaration of how we can all expect to face difficulties and tough times as we go through life. These tribulations so often steal peace from us and leave us upset and worried. Those who believe that the Christian life somehow makes everything nice and easy are just not listening carefully to the words of Jesus. The tribulation Jesus speaks of is for all of us.

Fortunately, Jesus gives us a third promise that brings great hope to all of us: "But take heart; I have overcome the world." Yes, we live in a world that is filled with tribulation. But Jesus firmly declared and then modeled on the cross and in the resurrection that he has indeed overcome the world. Peace is possible in the midst of tribulation because of the presence of the overcoming Christ in our lives. That gives us hope and even great joy, no matter what is happening in our lives.

Years ago, a little boy taught me much about this scripture. Kim and I, and our youngest son, David, were vacationing in North Carolina with the May family, who eventually became David's in-laws when he married their daughter, Natalie. The May family had a lot of children and they daily worked on memorizing the Bible in those years, even on vacation. The method they used would be to take a chapter and start at verses at the back, so that by the time they reached the beginning verses of the chapter, they really knew it. That week and the previous weeks, they had been working on memorizing John 16.

They started with verse one and each child took a portion and recited it as they moved around the room. The youngest was almost three-year-old Elijah, who was sitting on his dad's lap. He didn't have much of the chapter memorized at his age. But I noticed that as we got near the end of the chapter, he got more and more excited. By the time we got to verse 33, he was standing on his dad's lap with his hands outstretched and shouting out with the rest of his siblings the close of that verse, "But take heart, I have overcome the world!"

I wonder if we all can get as excited as that little boy about the promise of Jesus. Jesus is the overcomer. Regardless of the tribulations we face, the King of Kings is the overcomer. We can walk in peace in a life of stress and difficulty because that peace is in the heart of our

Overcoming God. Yes, tribulation is in this world. Yes, we can have peace. And yes, Jesus has overcome the world, which opens the door for his peace to mark our lives.

My Prayer

Thank you Lord for being our overcoming God! You knew better than any of us how difficult this world would be and how desperately we would need your peace. So you promised that we can have that peace if we would desire it and ask you for it. You overcame the dark powers of this world and provided your peace for us. Thank you, Lord! Pour your peace into me now that I might demonstrate your overcoming power to those around me.

Prayer Point

Today, commit to asking Jesus for his shalom (peace). Depend on his overcoming the world to provide the peace you need to also overcome whatever tribulation comes your way.

DAY 21
Stay in Perfect Peace

You will keep in perfect peace those whose minds are steadfast,
because they trust in you. (Isaiah 26:3)

I don't know about you, but perfect peace seems like an impossibility. With everything going on in the world around us, not to mention the confusion of thoughts within us, we wonder how such a promise could be made. It helps, of course, when it's God himself who made the statement. That puts this promise in a whole new light. It also helps for us to understand what is meant by perfect. Biblically speaking, perfection refers more to maturity or a level of completion. Here's the truth of the matter . . . God wants you to live in mature peace in your life and he is willing to commit to keep you in that place of peace.

The Prophet Isaiah gives us insight into how this works in a very practical way. The first and most important part is God's part. God commits to keep us in perfect peace. Without this commitment, it will not work. Peace is a gift of God, not simply something we work on. Jesus offered peace as something that came from him.

God's commitment to keep us in perfect peace is not without our part. We are to have our minds stayed on God. Perhaps an easier way of saying this is the New Testament command to fix our thoughts on Christ. What are you thinking about? What is your mind stayed on? It is impossible to have a mind filled with peace if our thoughts stray from the Lord. He keeps us in perfect peace when we fix our thoughts on him who is the source of peace. Over and over again, we are commanded to guard our hearts, to be careful what we are thinking about. Peace comes from a mind that is focused on God.

According to Isaiah, the third part of walking in perfect peace comes from trust. This is the combination of the nature of God and the work of man. We keep our minds fixed on God because we trust him. But we trust him because he has shown that he is worthy of all of our trust. He is the Eternal One, always faithful, always worthy of our trust. Because of who he is, we trust him. This brings peace.

I've never liked heights. Mountain climbing will never be my sport. I like mountains when I can sit in the valley and look up at them. One of the more traumatic, yet funny, experiences I had was with a group of pastors driving over a high mountain pass in the Rocky Mountains on the way to a staff retreat. It was a dangerous road with no guard rails and views that take your breath away. It took my breath away; I was terrified. The guys I was with knew I hated heights, so the conversation was about accidents on this road, and of course, we found ourselves going even faster than before. Then it happened. We were so high up that the bag of potato chips on the seat next to me, exploded with a loud bang. They had to scrape me off the ceiling! There was much laughter from the others.

I had no peace that day. My thoughts were on heights, and curves, and speeding cars, and potential accidents. Oh, and falling . . . lots of thoughts about falling. God doesn't step in to keep us in perfect peace when our mind is off somewhere else. Our lack of peace is no mystery. Just examine your thoughts. But there is a way to receive the amazing, mature peace of God and it comes from setting our minds upon him.

My Prayer

Lord Jesus, I am so grateful that you are not only a God of peace, but that you want to pass that peace to me. You literally commit yourself to keep me in peace. Help me to do my part. Help me through your Spirit to keep my mind stayed upon you and to trust you in every way.

Prayer Point

Today, choose to fix your mind and thoughts on Jesus, the Shalom Giver. Remind yourself of how he has been trustworthy in the past by thinking of those times he worked in amazing ways in your life.

Live at Peace with Everyone

If it is possible, as far as depends on you, live at peace with everyone. (Romans 12:18)

C hristians are the followers, the disciples, of the Prince of Peace. The peace of Christ has been offered to us and should mark our lives. So, it is not surprising that we hear the Apostle Paul challenge us to live at peace with everyone. That should be the standard operating procedure for every follower of Jesus. Those who are contentious and continually at strife with others are not following our God of all peace.

I love how practical this command is. The clear instruction that cannot and should not be avoided is that we, as followers of Jesus, should live at peace with everyone. But Paul realizes that it takes two to make that happen. One person by himself or herself can long for peace and work toward peace, but it takes the second person to agree to peace. So we are told, "as far as depends on you," live at peace. We cannot force someone to be at peace with us. There will be those who have decided to be our enemy, regardless of our desire for peace. We are not responsible for their determination to withhold peace from our relationship. We just live with the firm commitment to be at peace with everyone who will accept that peace.

The book of Genesis tells us a story of persistent pursuit of peace in the face of opposition. Isaac, the son of Abraham, moved near the Philistines during a time of famine in the land. God blessed Isaac's clan greatly and the Philistines became jealous and made Isaac and his people move further away. Moving to the Valley of Gerar, Isaac's servants dug a well to provide needed water. The Philistine herdsmen argued with Isaac's herdsmen and they moved farther away and dug another well. Again, the Philistines insisted that the water belonged to them. So, once again Isaac's clan moved again and dug a third well. This time, they were able to establish a dwelling place for their people.

This story in Genesis 26 ends with the King of the Philistines, Abimelek coming to Isaac and asking for a covenant of peace.

> Meanwhile, Abimelek had come to him from Gerar, with Ahuzzath his personal adviser and Phicol the commander of his forces. Isaac asked them, "Why have you come to me, since you were hostile to me and sent me away?"
>
> They answered, "We saw clearly that the LORD was with you; so we said, 'There ought to be a sworn agreement between us'—between us and you. Let us make a treaty with you that you will do us no harm, just as we did not harm you but always treated you well and sent you away peacefully. And now you are blessed by the LORD."
>
> Isaac then made a feast for them, and they ate and drank. Early the next morning the men swore an oath to each other. Then Isaac sent them on their way, and they went away peacefully.
>
> That day Isaac's servants came and told him about the well they had dug. They said, "We've found water!" He called it Shibah, and to this day the name of the town has been Beersheba. (Genesis 26:26-33)

We can learn much from Isaac about pursuing peace. Even though he had a position of wealth and power, he did not use that to try to dominate his neighbors. As opposition arose, he took every opportunity to choose the path of peace. At great inconvenience, he moved his flocks and family several times to avoid provoking the Philistines. When the Philistine leader who had created such tension came to him, instead of rejecting him, Isaac accepted the overtures of peace and created a covenant of peace with his neighbors. Persistent pursuit of peace often pays big dividends in the end.

Most of us have those who, for one reason or another, have chosen not to walk in peace with us. It might be a co-worker, a fellow student, a neighbor, or even a relative who just decides they don't like you and wants to make your life miserable. Like Isaac, we can choose to be a peacemaker, in so far as it depends upon us. That's what followers of Jesus do.

My Prayer

Lord, I hate conflict. I really do want to live in peace with everyone. Help me to pursue peace and not just be apathetic about uncomfortable situations. Show me how to do all that I can to live in peace with others. I want to reflect your peace to everyone I know.

Prayer Point

Ask the Lord to show you one person in your life with whom you need to work on developing a more peaceful relationship. Begin to pray for that person and situation, that Jesus would use you to be an agent of his peace.

DAY 23

Peace in Strange Places

Then the Spirit clothed Amasai, chief of the thirty, and he said, "We are yours, O David, and with you, O son of Jesse! Peace, peace to you, and peace to your helpers! For your God helps you." (1 Chronicles 12:18, ESV)

It was a tough time in Israel. In effect, it was civil war between those loyal to King Saul battling the young, but anointed, David and his small band. You never quite knew who to trust.

One day, a group of warriors from Benjamin and Judah came to David's stronghold to join him. David confronted them, wondering if they were for him or against him. It was at this tense point that the Spirit of God stepped in and spoke through Amasai. In that context of warriors signing up to do battle, the Spirit spoke a message of peace.

Peace comes sometimes in strange places. One of the best known and most loved stories of World War 1 tells of a special Christmas Eve when the bombing and shooting stopped and the Allied and Axis forces crossed into No Man's Land to talk and even share gifts with the men they had just been trying to kill. Christmas hymns were sung, some in German and some in English, but the message of peace was understood by all. The next day, it was war again, but for a few precious moments, peace ruled on the battlefield.

The peace that Amasai spoke to David was not talking about war stopping in Israel. It was more about the peace that David had because of God's presence with him, which then brought peace to those who allied themselves with David. It is peace in the midst of turmoil, not peace that comes from the absence of hostilities. It's a peace we all need to discover.

We so often feel that turmoil, conflict, or disorder is a sign that we have done something wrong. But we need to realize that these things are a part of what it means to live in this fallen world. Jesus, who modeled perfect peace for us, was so often surrounded by turmoil and attacks. He warned us that in this world, we would face tribulation. And yet, the peace of Christ comes to us regardless of the hectic, crazy world that surrounds us.

For us, as with David and Amasai, we must pay careful attention to the Spirit who speaks peace in the middle of war. The peace of God is not a matter of withdrawal from life or the avoidance of conflict. It is watching to see where God is moving and going where God is going. Amasai saw through the Spirit that God was with David and his helpers and that this was where peace was to be found. Yes, there still was hard fighting ahead and a throne to be won for David, but the presence of God with him ensured that God's peace would ultimately prevail.

My Prayer

Lord, help me to want to run after you, seeking your face always. That's where peace is to be found. Give me the strength to endure difficult times and to accept your peace while I am walking through those times. Help me to pay attention to the leading of your Spirit and to move always in your direction, being confident that your peace accompanies me on that path.

Prayer Point

Ask the Lord to show you what he is doing today, and how you are to cooperate in his activity.

Be at Peace with Him

---

*So then, dear friends, since you are looking forward to this, make
every effort to be found spotless, blameless and at peace with
him. (2 Peter 3:14)*

Many years ago, I was preaching a sermon series on the
Second Coming of Jesus. After one of the sermons, I was
shaking hands at the back of the church building and had
a fascinating conversation with one of our new members. She had
never been in church in her life and had just begun to get involved
with us. In complete innocence she asked me, "When Jesus comes
back, should we meet here at the church building?" Fighting back
an urge to laugh, I assured her that we wouldn't have to worry about
that. When Jesus came, he would immediately gather us to himself.

There is much confusion regarding the Second Coming of Jesus.
Some, like the dear woman from my church, have never heard good
teaching about this important topic. Most though, have never seriously
considered the Second Coming of Jesus and have collected in their
minds a wild assortment of beliefs and ideas that may or may not
match the teachings of Scripture. What will help us all are these
simple instructions from Peter on how we should live in anticipation
of Jesus' return.

First of all, though, Peter makes the assumption that Christians
are looking forward to the coming of Jesus. For many, I'm afraid, this
is an incorrect assumption. We too often find ourselves firmly at home
in this world, and not at all looking forward to Christ's return. I'm
convinced that one of the most important yet ignored biblical doctrines
is that of the imminent return of Jesus. The early Christians modeled
for us the power of living a life that looks eagerly for the return of
Jesus, while at the same time passionately living out the life of Jesus

in everyday acts of love and service. Are you looking forward to the return of Jesus?

With the Second Coming as a desire of our lives, Peter then tells us that we should be found spotless, blameless, and at peace with him when he returns. I love that Peter doesn't get caught up in controversies regarding timing and events but focuses on the lifestyle that ushers in Christ's return. Being spotless, blameless and at peace does not speak of perfection but of relationship. An intimate, right relationship with Jesus now will lead to looking forward to the face-to-face relationship of the Second Coming in the future.

The finished work of Christ upon the cross allows us to be without spot, without blame, and at peace with God. We cannot have these things apart from Jesus. But we must note that Peter commands us to make every effort to be found with these characteristics in our lives. We accept Christ and all that he is and offers, and then through his Spirit, we bring these attributes to fullness in our lives. Looking forward to his coming causes us to make every effort to be found practicing in our lives what it means to be spotless, blameless, and at peace with God.

My Prayer

Lord Jesus, I long for your return. Forgive me for getting too comfortable here in this world and forgetting the truth of your soon return. Show me how to live in a way that not only prepares me for your return, but also points others to you. I want to be spotless, blameless, and at peace with you when you appear in Glory.

Prayer Point

To train yourself to look forward to the Second Coming, each morning as you wake ask the Lord, "Is it today that you return?" Put the last prayer in Scripture on your lips each day: "Come Lord Jesus."

DAY 25

Speak Peace

I will listen to what God the LORD says; he promises peace to his people, his faithful servants—but let them not turn to folly. (Psalm 85:8)

While still in college, I began to be passionate about revival. I so wanted to experience the Lord's presence, not just in my life, but to see it in the Church. I didn't really know much about it then and I certainly didn't know how to pray for revival. I had one verse I retuned to again and again: "Will you not revive us again, that your people may rejoice in you?" (Psalm 85:6). It is fascinating to me, and a little sad, that in those early years, I never studied the rest of Psalm 85. It is really all about revival.

As I looked again at Psalm 85, I found this outline of revival teaching in the text of this psalm:

1. God was angry in the past, but restored his people.
2. God is currently angry and his people need revival.
3. It is time to pray and seek the Lord.
4. It is time to listen to the Lord.
5. God's answer is the peace of his presence.

The psalmist rightly moves from making his requests regarding revival to a time of silence in which he listens for the Lord's response. God's response, summed up in verse 8 is that he will speak peace to his people. When God receives our pleas for revival, he answers by speaking to us of peace. For most of us, that is not what we expect. However, we need to trust that the Father knows best and that if we are to see revival, we must listen to the Lord speak peace to his people.

Though the rest of Psalm 85 refers to peace, the clearest place is to jump to the life of Jesus and listen to his words of peace. In three powerful teachings, Jesus fulfilled the promise of Psalm 85:8 that he would speak peace to his saints.

Again Jesus said, "Peace be with you! As the Father has sent me, I am sending you." (John 20:21)

"I have told you these things, so that in me you may have peace. In this world you will have trouble. But take heart! I have overcome the world." (John 16:33)

"Peace I leave with you; my peace I give to you. I do not give to you as the world gives. Do not let your hearts be troubled and do not be afraid." (John 14:27)

The Apostle Paul takes this teaching of Jesus about peace and helps us understand why it must be understood as a basis for revival. "He came and preached peace to you who were far away and peace to those who were near" (Ephesians 2:17). The preaching of Jesus about peace was the heart of the gospel. Jesus came to bring peace, first of all between God and men, and then between men. There is no hope for revival until the finished work of Christ in establishing peace between God and men is accomplished first.

The cross of Christ brought peace to all who would receive. Paul said it this way: "For he himself is our peace, who has made the two groups one and has destroyed the barrier, the dividing wall of hostility, by setting aside in his flesh the law with its commands and regulations. His purpose was to create in himself one new humanity out of the two, thus making peace" (Ephesians 2:14-15).

When Christ is preached, peace at the deepest level becomes possible.

The question for us today is whether or not we, like the psalmist, have become quiet enough to hear the Lord speak peace to us. He will speak the peace that brings us into right relationship with God. Then he will speak the peace that brings us together as his children. His peace becomes a way of life for us that honors him and points people to the Christ who is still preaching peace to his people.

My Prayer

Lord, I thank you for your message of peace to us. That on the cross, you, in your flesh, broke down the dividing wall between us and the Father and between us as humans. You are our peace! I embrace your peace today and ask you to help me live that out in every aspect of my life.

Prayer Point

We often use the passage, "Be still and know that I am God" (Psalm 46:10). Add to that today, "Be still and listen to Jesus speak his peace to his saints." Ask Jesus to speak his shalom to you today.

Righteousness Is Sown in Peace

Peacemakers who sow in peace reap a harvest of righteousness.
(James 3:18)

The Bible is filled with instructions telling us that whatever we sow, we will reap. In the gardening world, my wife and I discovered that truth two years ago. We went to the nursery to buy zucchini plants. Even though they are prolific, we wanted a number of plants because we use zucchini in lots of ways. It was a good year and the plants took off with good growth. It's when the zucchini started to form that we began to question things. Most of the vegetables were obviously zucchini, but some of the produce were rounded and much larger. By the time they turned orange, we knew that about half of our zuchinnis were, in fact, pumpkins. Every single plant was marked zucchini by the nursery. Regardless of what we thought we were planting, what we sowed, we reaped.

In the very practical book of James, chapter 3 closes in verse 18 with a similar challenge regarding sowing and reaping. Verses 13-18 are all about the desirability of wisdom, and James contrasts earthy wisdom with heavenly wisdom. Verse 17 describes the beauty of heavenly wisdom: "But the wisdom from above is first pure, then peaceable, gentle, open to reason, full of mercy and good fruits, impartial and sincere." The harvest of such righteous behaviors comes when you sow in peace by those who make peace.

This commendation fits well with the admonition of Jesus in the Beatitudes: "Blessed are the peacemakers, for they will be called children of God" (Matthew 5:9). Jesus himself is described in a similar way by the Prophet Nahum: "Look, there on the mountains, the feet of one who brings good news, who proclaims peace!" (Nahum 1:15). Those who make peace have walked with Jesus and learned of his peace. Now they can bring that peace to others.

James puts this into a picture that helps us understand our role. We want to see the wisdom that comes from above that brings righteousness. This harvest of righteousness comes from the steady planting of peace by those who are following Jesus. It's an interesting picture that most of us have not grasped. We speak peace, live peace, work for peace, and literally follow the Prince of Peace as peacemakers. That is a sowing of peace. What this passage does for us though, is point out the added, even perhaps ultimate result of sowing peace. Heavenly wisdom comes that is desperately needed in our world. It is wisdom that is pure, peaceable, gentle, reasonable, merciful, impartial and sincere. That's quite a harvest!

I love how this passage of Scripture takes peace from simply being a personal characteristic and make it a powerful instrument in expanding the kingdom of God on earth. It's no longer just about us trying to experience peace, but now, as those who are sowing into others' lives, we are seeing a harvest of righteousness that exalts Jesus and empowers his followers for greater effectiveness. We are peacemakers who are changing the world through the power of the Holy Spirit, who is leading us to sow peace wherever we go.

My Prayer

I thank you Lord, that I am privileged to follow you as the Prince of Peace. You have called me to be a peacemaker in my own life, family, congregation, and culture. Would you help me to keep my eyes fixed on you that I might always be one who sows peace wherever I find myself? May your Spirit take my sowing efforts and produce an amazing harvest of righteousness!

Prayer Point

Ask Jesus to open your eyes to see the opportunities he brings to you where you can sow peace into the life of someone else.

Life and Peace

So letting your sinful nature control your mind leads to death.
But letting the Spirit control your mind leads to life and peace.
(Romans 8:6, NLT)

Whenen you read the above passage from Romans, it seems like a very clear and easy choice. Death . . . or life and peace. But when it comes to practical choices, in the middle of the stressful seasons of life, it isn't that clear. Christians who don't want to let the sinful nature control their minds can find that happening, often without realizing it. When peace seems to be elusive, it's a good bet that the Spirit is not in control of our minds. My wife, Kim, shares a very personal story of how easily that can happen:

Recently, I unintentionally robbed God of control over several situations in my life. I succumbed to the lie of the enemy that I could find solutions to some devastating family issues. My two sisters were and are, as I write, very ill—one physically and the other mentally. My sweet, elderly mother is struggling to maintain her memory and is losing both her eyesight and her hearing. On top of this, they all live almost 2,000 miles away from me. One sister can barely talk, the other won't talk, and my mother can't understand what I am saying over the phone because of her hearing impairment. I felt so crushed under the weight of loss that I was desperate to make my world and theirs right again. Three very special women in my life had been cut off from me within the span of a few months and somehow, I had to fix it all! I researched solutions and talked to people who could help and even made seven trips to California within one year. I prayed selfishly for God to do what I wanted rather than for what he might be trying to do in their lives and mine. After all the stress and anxiety, I was able to do a few things to help . . . but I couldn't really "fix" any of it.

Then, without warning, my husband was diagnosed with stage 4 cancer. *Really, God?* It was then that the Holy Spirit showed me how my sinful nature had completely taken over, robbing my mind of the life and peace mentioned in Romans 8. He gently showed me that I needed to surrender the rest of my ailing family to him, so that I could walk through cancer with Dave. I could stay in touch, encourage and pray for them, but I couldn't "fix" anything. I simply had to be dependent and lay all of the stresses and anxieties of these issues before the feet of the One who created all of these people I love so much. I began to learn how suffering leads to spiritual maturity. Leaving burdens in his hands, setting my prayers upon what his solutions might be, and obediently letting go of the control over these circumstances has been very humbling. But being transformed by the renewing of my mind through the grace of God, I have been led once again into life and peace . . . even in the midst of a cancer battle! Trusting the Holy Spirit to deal with circumstances beyond my control has been very freeing and has brought rest and peace into my soul.

There is a key word in Romans 8:6 that appears twice: "letting." It is used in the context of allowing either your sinful nature or the Spirit to control your mind. The clear implication of Scripture is that you get to choose who will control your mind. The result of your choice will be either death or life and peace. This isn't a small choice but something that can forever change the direction of your life.

As Kim's testimony shows, when life is out of control, we can so easily forget to relinquish our desire to seize control rather than trust God to bring his "rightness" to our circumstances. We feel compelled and overwhelmed and as a result, we forget to choose that which brings life and peace. When we decide instead to let the Spirit control our minds, we are able to lay aside the anxieties of life and choose God's peace. On a very practical level, perhaps the easiest way to do this is simply to ask the Lord for his help.

My Prayer

Lord, help me today to let your Spirit control my mind. It is so easy for me to step in and try to fix or control things that are beyond me. My trust is in you. I choose to let you control my thought and desires today and each day of my life.

Prayer Point

Today, ask Jesus for help to enable you to let His Holy Spirit control your mind so you might experience life and peace.

DAY 28

The Peace Process

For the kingdom of God is not a matter of eating and drinking, but of righteousness, peace and joy in the Holy Spirit, because anyone who serves Christ in this way is pleasing to God and receives human approval. Let us therefore make every effort to do what leads to peace and to mutual edification. (Romans 14:17-19)

God certainly makes it clear that peace is a high priority in the Kingdom. From Old Testament teaching and example, to the life and message of Jesus, to the clear teaching of the New Testament epistles, peace is consistently presented as a central focus of the desire of God for his people. It is of such importance that one of the titles for Jesus is Prince of Peace.

Though humans have not done well in living out peace, the high value that God places on peace has made its way in our collective psyche. Some of our best thinkers and writers have written about peace. Here are a few short quotes from a diverse group:

Peace is a daily, a weekly, a monthly process, gradually changing opinions, slowly eroding old barriers, quietly building new structures. —John F. Kennedy

When I say it's you I like, I'm talking about that part of you that knows that life is far more than anything you can ever see or hear or touch. That deep part of you that allows you to stand for those things without which humankind cannot survive. Love that conquers hate, peace that rises triumphant over war, and justice that proves more powerful than greed. —Fred Rogers

We plant seeds that will flower as results in our lives, so best to remove the weeds of anger, avarice, envy and doubt, that peace and abundance may manifest for all. —Dorothy Day

We look forward to the time when the power to love will replace the love of power. Then will our world know the blessing of peace.

—William Gladstone

I wonder when the Church will begin to put such a high value on peace. All too often, we Christians are seen as those who fuss and fight over little things. Church fights and splits are all too common and certainly do not present a message of peace to our culture. If we want to continue to be a biblical people, it is time to get serious about being a people of peace.

Today's text gives a message of peace that simply cannot be ignored. Paul says with apostolic authority that the Kingdom of God is a matter of peace. Because of that, we are to make every effort to do what leads to peace. Can you imagine a church fellowship where this is taught and modeled? Our assemblies should be marked by an atmosphere of peace whenever we gather.

It is time that church leaders begin to teach and expect peace as a characteristic of corporate Christianity. But for that to happen, all of us need to begin pursuing peace within us as part of what it means to walk with Jesus. We must take to heart Paul's instruction that we are to "make every effort to do what leads to peace."

My Prayer

Lord, I thank you that the very angels sang of peace when you were born. You have built peace into the gospel message and made it a pillar of your kingdom. May your Church begin to reflect your peace in radical ways in the way we treat one another. Teach us to passionately pursue peace in ways that demonstrate your life of peace within us.

Prayer Point

Ask the Lord to make peace a dominant characteristic of the congregation where you worship.

DAY 29

Peace at All Times

Now may the Lord of peace himself give you peace at all times in every way. The Lord be with all of you. (2 Thessalonians 3:16)

I love the various names given to Jesus in Scripture. The Lord of Peace is one of my favorite names. It speaks to his character as well as his mission. Jesus demonstrated peace consistently in his life. Then on the cross, he accomplished the greatest peace-giving mission on the planet by tearing down the dividing wall both between God and men and that which divides men from each other. His name, Lord of Peace, fits perfectly.

Paul takes this powerful name and makes it into a blessing for us to use, not only by accepting it into our own lives, but by sharing it with others. Before you begin to bless others, the first thing that must happen is accepting the Lord's peace in a personal and practical way into your own life. What Jesus wants to give us is pervasive peace. Listen to how Paul says it: "give you peace at all times and in every way." No exceptions to this gift. It's not a matter of peace when we feel like it or when everything is going fine. It is peace at all times and in every way. That is what each of us may have if we accept the gift of peace from Christ.

Then we notice that the word "may" at the beginning makes this a blessing which we can then pray over others. Whom do you know who needs peace at all times in every way? Just about everyone you know? We need to have the courage to speak this blessing over others. It is a gift of peace that should not be kept to ourselves. Giving this blessing doesn't require you bow your head or close your eyes. Memorize it and speak it over those who need it. Perhaps you could simply write out a blessing of peace and send it to them by mail or email.

The key to this peace is found in the last sentence of this verse, "The Lord be with all of you." It is the Lord's presence that brings and assures peace. Perhaps one of the most powerful ways you can experience peace is simply to picture the Lord sitting with you. Allow the sense of his presence to change your emotions and feelings. This experience is not strange; you are simply acting on the truth of Scripture. Colossians 1:27 reminds us that Christ in us is the hope of glory. Spend time aware of his presence and watch his peace flow into you.

There are several biblical blessings of peace that Kim and I like to pray, but our favorite is what is often called the Aaronic blessing in Numbers 6:24-26, "The LORD bless you and keep you; the LORD make his face shine on you and be gracious to you; the LORD turn his face toward you and give you peace."

Kim began praying that over our youngest son, David, every night from his youngest days. Because the blessing was such an important part of his life, the night before he was to be married, our 6'5" son came into our bedroom, knelt down by the bed and asked for his blessing of peace. Blessing others makes a real difference in their lives.

My Prayer

Lord Jesus, I thank you that your presence brings peace. You are my Lord of Peace and I gratefully receive your gift of peace at all times and in every way. Show me how to bless others with your peace.

Prayer Point

Each day, select someone who you might bless with peace. Whether you see him or her in person and can physically bless him/her, or you have to send the person a text or email, make sure you pass along the peace the Lord has given to you.

DAY 30

Live in Peace

Finally, brothers and sisters, rejoice! Strive for full restoration, encourage one another, be of one mind, live in peace. And the God of love and peace will be with you. (2 Corinthians 13:11)

Today is the last day of a 30-day journey that we've taken together in praying for the shalom of Jesus. My journey as the author likely took longer than yours and had far more twists and turns than I ever dreamed possible. My shocking stage 4 cancer diagnosis just a few weeks into beginning the book certainly was a challenge to walking in Christ's peace.

As I finish this book, I am also finishing my fourth cycle of intense chemo, during which I am hospitalized. It is working well and the medical personnel are pleased with how I am handling treatment. I'm grateful for their great care, but I'm also careful to tell them often that they are being assisted in their work in unusual and amazing ways through the power of God. I continually tell them that there are literally thousands of Christians who are praying for me and that we have experienced the healing and protective power of the Lord throughout the treatments.

The book on peace is coming to an end, but I don't know the end of the story for me personally. I believe that God is working to bring healing to me. I fully expect to write more books and spend more years teaching on prayer. But my days are in the Lord's hands, and I am content in knowing that.

What I do want to share is the way the Lord has taught Kim and me about his peace through these days. A stage 4 cancer diagnosis typically takes one's peace away; however, in many ways, it has restored our peace. The seriousness of the cancer has taught us to trust in the Lord and not in ourselves. Because of this, peace has been deeply rooted and well-established in our hearts. The life or death nature of my situation has brought us into deeper intimacy with Christ and his presence brings ultimate tranquility. Of course there are difficult times, but the journey has pushed us more and more into the Word of God. That strengthens our resolve to continually seek the peace that replaces stress, anger, confusion and doubt with a joy-filled trust. Perhaps more than anything, being transparent about our situation has brought our brothers and sisters in Christ around us in astonishing ways, filling us with gratefulness and calm, peace-filled hearts.

Kim and I have been in awe of the demonstrations of love that have been shown by Christians from around the world as they have heard about my health issues. So many have prayed, given financially, written or spoken words of encouragement, brought meals, and visited. God's peace has been shown to us through so many acts of love. The fun part has been being able to pass that along.

Every third week I spend in the hospital getting some intense chemo. We have developed a wonderful relationship with so many medical workers. We share and pray, and laugh and cry with these great caregivers. Our commitment to walk in the peace of Christ seems to draw them to us. Our lives have been enriched as we have ministered the peace of Christ to them. It seems to us that we have discovered the reality of Paul's instruction to the Church in 2 Corinthians 13:11, "Finally, brothers and sisters, rejoice! Strive for full restoration, encourage one another, be of one mind, live in peace. And the God of love and peace will be with you."

In the midst of the uncertainty of life lived with cancer, we have discovered the peace that is totally separated from our circumstances. It is peace in the midst of pain and discomfort. Above all, it is about the presence of Christ. Where Jesus is, there is life and peace. Drawing near to Him each day brings the peace that passes all understanding.

You can live and walk in this peace, too. Simply call on Jesus, the Peace-Giver. Lay everything that is stressing you before him, and let the shalom of Jesus envelop you!

My Prayer

Prince of Peace, I bow before you in worship and adoration today. Thank you for giving me yobur peace in the middle of my struggles and trials. Your peace is so amazing. I draw near to your awesome presence and there I find my peace.

Prayer Point

Commit today to draw near to the Lord where his peace will be found.

Epilogue

Thank you for joining me on this journey to the shalom of Jesus. Personally it has been a very real journey with lots of twists and turns. Most of this book was written while in a hospital bed, fighting stage 4 Mantle Cell Lymphoma. While considered an incurable cancer, medical research has allowed it to be more of a chronic disease for many. The good news for me is that as I finished this book, I moved into remission!

I don't believe God gives people cancer. But he is never far from us in the midst of the life or death struggle that so often marks cancer. Inviting him into the process is always a better approach and always brings his peace. We saw that happen again and again during these days. What was exciting for Kim and me was that the Lord's peace didn't just envelope us, but it also touched so many others as we prayed and tried to demonstrate his peace. From nurses up close, to Facebook friends afar, we saw God bring glory to himself by pouring out his peace upon us in the midst of trial.

God so often takes what the enemy intends for evil and turns it around to advance his kingdom. He does that more often when we cooperate with how he is working. We can say, with absolute integrity, that we know of thousands of believers who prayed for us. Kim and I chose to talk often in the hospital about the many who were praying for us, trying to encourage the faith of believers around us. Many of you reading this book provided the prayer support that both brought healing and touched so many lives.

The Lord also taught me much about not trying to see how much I could accomplish on my own, but about depending wholly upon him. I was amazed at how much effective ministry, whether writing, videos, conference calls, or times of deep prayer, could happen from a hospital bed. It's not the place or way I would have chosen, but the Lord demonstrated his sovereign power over any and all circumstances. As I move away from a hospital bed, back into more traditional ministry,

I want to maintain that dependence on the Lord that marks truly effective service.

Like all of us, my future is in the Lord's hands. Whether God has permanently healed me, or my cancer is simply in remission and one day returns, I do not know. What I do know is that Jesus has given me peace.

This peace is available to all of his followers. This peace transforms us from the inside and allows us to overcome any circumstance in this life. It's a wonderful day by day journey with the Prince of Peace!

Live in Peace,

Dave Butts

Scriptures about Peace

Below are each day's scriptures. If you are in the midst of a trial that is robbing you of peace, we recommend reading and praying through these verses as a way of boosting your faith and of surrendering your life to Jesus, the Prince of Peace.

In peace I will lie down and sleep, for you alone, LORD, make me dwell in safety. (Psalm 4:8)

For he himself is our peace, who has made the two groups one and has destroyed the barrier, the dividing wall of hostility, by setting aside in his flesh the law with its commands and regulations. His purpose was to create in himself one new humanity out of the two, thus making peace. (Ephesians 2:14-15)

Peace I leave with you; my peace I give you. I do not give to you as the world gives. Do not let your hearts be troubled and do not be afraid. (John 14:27)

"Do not be afraid, you who are highly esteemed," he said. "Peace! Be strong now; be strong." When he spoke to me, I was strengthened and said, "Speak, my lord, since you have given me strength." (Daniel 10:19)

The God of peace will soon crush Satan under your feet. The grace of our Lord Jesus be with you. (Romans 16:20)

Even though I walk through the valley of the shadow of death, I will fear no evil, for you are with me; your rod and your staff, they comfort me. (Psalm 23:4, ESV)

The LORD gives strength to his people; the LORD blesses his people with peace. (Psalm 29:11)

For God is not a God of confusion but of peace. (1 Corinthians 14:33, ESV)

Grace, mercy and peace from God the Father and from Jesus Christ, the Father's Son, will be with us in truth and love. (2 John 1:3)

Again Jesus said, "Peace be with you! As the Father has sent me, I am sending you." (John 20:21)

And the peace of God, which transcends all understanding, will guard your hearts and your minds in Christ Jesus. (Philippians 4:7)

He came and preached peace to you who were far away and peace to those who were near. (Ephesians 2:17)

So then, dear friends, since you are looking forward to this, make every effort to be found spotless, blameless and at peace with him. (2 Peter 3:14)

But the fruit of the Spirit is love, joy, peace, forbearance, kindness, goodness, faithfulness. (Galatians 5:22)

Turn from evil and do good; seek peace and pursue it. (Psalm 34:14)

If the home is deserving, let your peace rest on it; if it is not, let your peace return to you. (Matthew 10:13)

"If you, even you, had only known on this day what would bring you peace—but now it is hidden from your eyes." (Luke 19:42)

Let the peace of Christ rule in your hearts, since as members of one body you were called to peace. And be thankful. (Colossians 3:15)

That day when evening came, he said to his disciples, "Let us go over to the other side." Leaving the crowd behind, they took him along, just as he was, in the boat. There were also other boats with him. A furious squall came up, and the waves broke over the boat, so that it was nearly swamped. Jesus was in the stern, sleeping on a cushion. The disciples woke him and said to him, "Teacher, don't you care if we drown?" He got up, rebuked the wind and said to the waves, "Quiet! Be still!" Then the wind died down and it was completely calm. He said to his disciples, "Why are you so afraid? Do you still have no faith?" They were terrified and asked each other, "Who is this? Even the wind and the waves obey him!" (Mark 4:35-41)

"So that I come again to my father's house in peace, then the Lord shall be my God." (Genesis 28:21, ESV)

"I have said these things to you, that in me you may have peace. In the world you will have tribulation. But take heart; I have overcome the world." (John 16:33, ESV)

You will keep in perfect peace those whose minds are steadfast, because they trust in you. (Isaiah 26:3)

If it is possible, as far as depends on you, live at peace with everyone. (Romans 12:18)

Then the Spirit clothed Amasai, chief of the thirty, and he said, "We are yours, O David, and with you, O son of Jesse! Peace, peace to you, and peace to your helpers! For your God helps you." (1 Chronicles 12:18, ESV)

I will listen to what God the LORD says; he promises peace to his people, his faithful servants—but let them not turn to folly. (Psalm 85:8)

Peacemakers who sow in peace reap a harvest of righteousness. (James 3:18)

So letting your sinful nature control your mind leads to death. But letting the Spirit control your mind leads to life and peace. (Romans 8:6, NLT)

For the kingdom of God is not a matter of eating and drinking, but of righteousness, peace and joy in the Holy Spirit, because anyone who serves Christ in this way is pleasing to God and receives human approval. Let us therefore make every effort to do what leads to peace and to mutual edification. (Romans 14:17-19)

Now may the Lord of peace himself give you peace at all times in every way. The Lord be with all of you. (2 Thessalonians 3:16)

Finally, brothers and sisters, rejoice! Strive for full restoration, encourage one another, be of one mind, live in peace. And the God of love and peace will be with you. (2 Corinthians 13:11)

Bless Others with Peace!

If you enjoyed and were blessed by *Prayer, Peace and the Presence of God*, why not encourage your friends with this powerful resource? Or encourage your congregation to pray through this together.

Buy multiple copies and save at prayershop.org! Available wherever you purchase your Christian books, on ebook, or at prayershop.org.

PRAYERSHOP PUBLISHING

prayershop.org • (812) 238-5504

ADDITIONAL BOOKS
BY DAVE BUTTS

All books are available in e-book, through normal Christian book distribution sources and at prayershop.org.

PRAYER INITIATIVES

Asleep in the Land of Nod: Thirty Days to Awaken the Church is prayer devotional that focuses on spiritual revival of the Church.

Revolution on Your Knees: 30 Days of Prayer for Neighbors and Nations is an outreach-oriented prayer devotional to get people focused on praying for God's Kingdom to grow around them.

Vertical with Jesus: A 30-Day Journey to Impact Kingdom Living is a more in-depth prayer devotional that includes action steps for the reader to go deeper in their relationship with Jesus.

Desperate for Change: 40 Days of Prayer for America is designed to get individuals and churches praying God's purposes over our nation.

BIBLE STUDIES

Pray Like the King: Lessons from the Prayers of Israel's Kings looks at seven prayers of Kings of Israel and one of the King of Kings and from them provides insights into how to pray more effectively.

The Devil Goes to Church: Combating the Everyday Attacks of Satan provides six lessons that helps the user recognize and combat the common ways Satan attacks a church.

OTHER BOOKS

Forgotten Power: A Simple Theology for a Praying Church explains from scripture the importance of prayer in the life of a church.

Prayer and the End of Days: Praying God's Purposes in Troubled Times will challenge and encourage the user to pray with insight and discernment amid the difficult days in which we find ourselves.

With One Cry: A Renewed Challenge to Pray for America will encourage and equip the reader to pray in an effective way God's purposes over our nation.

When God Shows Up: Essays on Revival is a collection of articles Dave has written on revival in the Church and spiritual awakening.

PRAYERCONNECT

Connecting to the Heart of Christ through Prayer

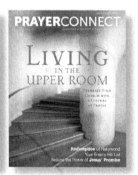

A QUARTERLY MAGAZINE DESIGNED TO:

Equip prayer leaders and pastors with tools to disciple their congregations.

Connect intercessors with the growing worldwide prayer movement.

Mobilize believers to pray God's purposes for their church, city and the nations.

Each issue of *Prayer Connect* includes:
- Practical articles to equip and inspire your prayer life.
- Helpful prayer tips and proven ideas.
- News of prayer movements around the world.
- Theme articles exploring important prayer topics.
- Connections to prayer resources available online.

Print subscription: $24.99
(includes digital version)

Digital subscription: $19.99

Church Prayer Leaders Network membership: $30 (includes print, digital, and CPLN membership benefits)

Subscribe now.
Order at prayerconnect.net or call 800-217-5200.

PRAYERCONNECT *is sponsored by: America's National Prayer Committee, Denominational Prayer Leaders Network and The International Prayer Council.*